These Are My Senses

What Can I Hear?

Joanna Issa

Raintree is an imprint of Capstone Global Library Limited, a company incorporated in England and Wales having its registered office at 7 Pilgrim Street, London, EC4V 6LB – Registered company number: 6695582

www.raintreepublishers.co.uk
myorders@raintreepublishers.co.uk

Text © Capstone Global Library Limited 2015
First published in hardback in 2014
The moral rights of the proprietor have been asserted.

Edited by Siân Smith
Designed by Richard Parker and Peggie Carley
Picture research by Tracy Cummins
Production by Victoria Fitzgerald
Originated by Capstone Global Library Ltd
Printed and bound in China by RR Donnelley Asia

ISBN 978 1 406 28370 9
18 17 16 15 14
10 9 8 7 6 5 4 3 2 1

British Library Cataloguing in Publication Data
A full catalogue record for this book is available from the British Library.

Acknowledgements
We would like to thank the following for permission to reproduce photographs: Alamy: © Francois Werli, 7, © Tetra Images, 17; Corbis: Blend Images/Jamie Grill/© JGI, 10, © Yang Liu, 9; Dreamstime: © Carlosphotos, 8, 21 left; Shutterstock: © aceshot1, 12, © Borislav Borisov, 6, 21 right, 22 right, back cover, © Damien Richard, 14, © Digital Storm, 4, 22 left, © jctabb, 16, 20 right, © Kalmatsuy Tatyana, 15, © Lisajsh, 13, © marco mayer, 5, © Martin Novak, 19, © Sergey Lavrentev, 18, 20 left; Veer: Olly, 11.

Cover photograph reproduced with permission of Getty Images: Flickr Open/Geri Lavrov.

Every effort has been made to contact copyright holders of material reproduced in this book. Any omissions will be rectified in subsequent printings if notice is given to the publisher.

Contents

What can I hear?

I hear a **loud** siren.

I have to cover my ears.

I hear a **quiet** sound.

A bird is quiet.

I hear fireworks.

I have to cover my ears.

I hear a quiet sound.

Rain is quiet.

I hear a drum.

I have to cover my ears.

I hear a quiet sound.

A cat is quiet.

I hear thunder.

I have to cover my ears.

I hear a quiet sound.

A whisper is quiet.

Quiz: Spot the difference

Can you find the loud sounds?

The thunder and the fireworks are loud.
The whisper and the bird are quiet.

Picture glossary

 **loud**

 **quiet**

Index

Notes for teachers and parents

BEFORE READING

Building background:

Ask children to close their eyes and imagine a plane flying overhead. Would they call this sound loud or quiet? Then ask them to rub their hands gently on their shirt sleeves. Is the sound loud or quiet? Ask children how they hear sounds.

AFTER READING

Recall and reflection:

What sounds are loud (siren, fireworks, drum, thunder)? What sounds are quiet (a bird singing, a cat purring, a whisper)? What do the children in the book do when they hear loud sounds? What do we have to do to hear quiet sounds?

Sentence knowledge:

Ask children to look at page 13. How many sentences are on this page?
How can they tell?

Word knowledge (phonics):

Encourage children to point at the word *hear* on page 4. Sound out the two phonemes in the word *h/ear*. Ask children to sound out each phoneme as they point at the letters and then blend the sounds together to make the word *hear*. Challenge them to say some words that rhyme with *hear* (ear, deer, gear, near).

Word recognition:

Ask children to point to the word *sound* on page 10.
On which other page can they find this word (page 14)?

EXTENDING IDEAS

Put some percussion instruments on a table (tambourine, drum, cymbals, maracas). Let children listen to the sounds of each instrument and talk about whether the sound is loud or quiet. Cover up the instruments. Choose a child from the group, and tell the others to cover their eyes. Remove one of the instruments and ask the child to play the instrument. Can the rest of the class guess what instrument is being played? Tell the child to play the instrument very quietly at first and then to gradually get louder and louder. Do the other children need to cover their ears?

In this book

Topic

hearing and senses

Sentence stems

1. I hear a loud _____.

2. I _____ cover my ears.

3. _____ is quiet.

High-frequency words

a

have

I

is

my

to